TURTLE FARMING
IN THE
TORRES STRAIT, 1970S

By Bertha Natanielu

Illustrated by Mila Aydingoz

We respect and honour Aboriginal and Torres Strait Islander Elders past, present and future. We acknowledge the stories, traditions and living cultures of Aboriginal and Torres Strait Islander peoples on this land and commit to building a brighter future together.

Library For All Ltd.

When I was younger, I left Thursday Island for a while. I jumped on an Applied Ecology boat and did some turtle farming on the islands that had it.

Masig Island

Badu
Island

Horn Island

CAPE YORK

4

Bramble Cay

Erub Island

Mer Island

The turtle farms were on Mer (Murray Island), Erub (Darnley Island), Masig (Yorke Island) and Badu (Mulgrave Island).

On Raine Island, there was a turtle hatchery. Green turtles still go there every year to lay their eggs.

Raine Island

On the farms, they had small tanks where they grew the turtles from eggs.

After a while, we would put the turtles in larger tanks until they were big enough to be sold or released.

As we went around the islands, we would pick up students from James Cook University. They would work as crew or help the scientists from Applied Ecology with their research.

The students would study turtles
all around Bramble Cay.

After six months, we would drop them off at Horn Island and take new students out to see the turtles.

Raine Island is a special island. It has an old tower, which was built by convicts. The tower used to help ships that passed through our strait. It is called the Beacon. Before it was built, there were a lot of shipwrecks.

I was the only Island woman who went to Raine Island at that time.

In 1980-1981, Applied Ecology stopped turtle farming and moved onto crocodile farming in the Pormpuraaw Aboriginal community on Gulf Country.

This was a great time in my life when I was working for Applied Ecology. I learned so much about turtles and eco systems.

Turtle farming in the Torres Strait

Turtles have always been important to people in the Torres Strait Islands. For some people, the turtle is considered sacred. It is also hunted for food.

In 1973, the Australian government set up a company called Applied Ecology Pty Ltd, which studied marine turtles and worked with local people to build sustainable turtle farms. Staff and students from James Cook University's School of Veterinary Science travelled around the islands with the company to assist with research; they were working on ways to maximise efficient turtle breeding for market.

After five years, Applied Ecology determined that the slow rate of turtle growth and high farming costs meant the system was not economically viable. They recommended further research into free-range farming. At the time, it was estimated that 10 000 turtles were consumed in the region each year.

At the same time, Applied Ecology established a crocodile farm at the Edward River Mission in the Gulf of Carpentaria. This area is now known as Pormpuraaw. As turtle farming declined, the company increased its focus on the crocodile market.

Thursday Island resident Bertha Natanielu worked with Applied Ecology Pty Ltd in the 1970s. This is her story about that time.

Sources:

- Jan O'Connell, Australian Food Timeline, australianfoodtimeline.com.au, viewed 2024.

- JM Thomson, 'The Turtle farming project in Torres Strait – North Queensland', Joint SPC-NMFS Workshop on Marine Turtles in the tropical Pacific Islands, 1979.

You can use these questions to talk about this book with your family, friends and teachers.

What did you learn from this book?

Describe this book in one word. Funny? Scary? Colourful? Interesting?

How did this book make you feel when you finished reading it?

What was your favourite part of this book?

About the author

Bertha Natanielu was born in Cairns but lives on Thursday Island, where she loves going camping with her friends and family. Bertha's favourite story as a child was *The Famous Five*, and her Our Yarning contributions are based off her own experiences.

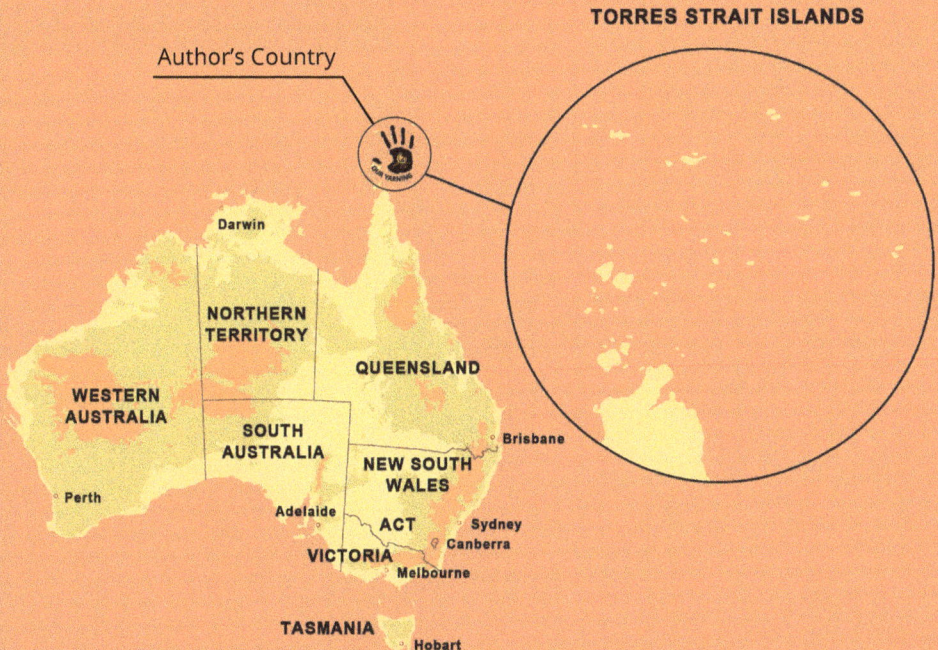

TORRES STRAIT ISLANDS

Author's Country

Darwin

NORTHERN
TERRITORY

QUEENSLAND

WESTERN
AUSTRALIA

SOUTH
AUSTRALIA

NEW SOUTH
WALES

Brisbane

Perth

Adelaide

ACT

Sydney

Canberra

VICTORIA

Melbourne

TASMANIA

Hobart

Our Yarning

The Our Yarning collection aligns with the Australian Curriculum through the Cross-Curriculum Priorities — Aboriginal and Torres Strait Islander Histories and Cultures. The collection provides an authentic opportunity for learning and embedding Aboriginal and Torres Strait Islander perspectives because it is written by Aboriginal and Torres Strait Islander people.

We know that children learn better, and enjoy reading more, when they see themselves in the stories, characters and illustrations of the books they read.

To download the app, visit the Google Play Store or Apple Store and search 'Our Yarning'.

libraryforall.org

You're reading Middle Primary

Learner – Beginner readers

Start your reading journey with short words, big ideas and plenty of pictures.

Level 1 – Rising readers

Raise your reading level with more words, simple sentences and exciting images.

Level 2 – Eager readers

Enjoy your reading time with familiar words, but complex sentences.

Level 3 – Progressing readers

Develop your reading skills with creative stories and some challenging vocabulary.

Level 4 – Fluent readers

Step up your reading skills with playful narratives, new words and fun facts.

Middle Primary – Curious readers

Discover your world through science and stories.

Upper Primary – Adventurous readers

Explore your world through science and stories.

Turtle Farming in the Torres Strait, 1970s

First published 2024

Published by Library For All Ltd
Email: info@libraryforall.org
URL: libraryforall.org

Our Yarning logo design by Jason Lee, Bidjipidji Art

Original illustrations by Mila Aydingoz

Turtle Farming in the Torres Strait, 1970s
Natanielu, Bertha
ISBN: 978-1-923207-33-2
SKU04393